TIME® LIFE BOOKS

Other Publications:

HISTORY
Our American Century
What Life Was Like
The American Story
Voices of the Civil War
The American Indians
Lost Civilizations
Mysteries of the Unknown
Time Frame
The Civil War
Cultural Atlas

COOKING
Weight Watchers® Smart Choice Recipe Collection
Great Taste~Low Fat
Williams-Sonoma Kitchen Library

DO IT YOURSELF
Total Golf
How to Fix It
The Time-Life Complete Gardener
Home Repair and Improvement
The Art of Woodworking

TIME-LIFE KIDS
Student Library
Library of First Questions and Answers
A Child's First Library of Learning
I Love Math
Nature Company Discoveries
Understanding Science & Nature

SCIENCE/NATURE
Voyage Through the Universe

For information on and a full description of
any of the Time-Life Books series listed above,
please call 1-800-621-7026 or write:

Reader Information
Time-Life Customer Service
P.O. Box C-32068
Richmond, Virginia 23261-2068

This volume is one of a series that chronicles
in full the events of the Second World War.

WORLD WAR II · TIME-LIFE BOOKS · ALEXANDRIA, VIRGINIA

BY RUSSELL MILLER
AND THE EDITORS OF TIME-LIFE BOOKS

THE COMMANDOS

Time-Life Books is a division of Time Life Inc.

TIME LIFE INC.
PRESIDENT and CEO: George Artandi

TIME-LIFE BOOKS
PRESIDENT: Stephen R. Frary
PUBLISHER/MANAGING EDITOR: Neil Kagan
VICE PRESIDENT, MARKETING: Joseph A. Kuna

WORLD WAR II

DIRECTOR, NEW PRODUCT DEVELOPMENT:
Elizabeth D. Ward
DIRECTOR OF MARKETING: Pamela R. Farrell

Dust Jacket Design: Barbara M. Sheppard

Editorial Staff for *The Commandos*
Editor: Thomas H. Flaherty Jr.
Senior Editors: Anne Horan, Henry Woodhead
Designer: Herbert H. Quarmby
Chief Researcher: Philip Brandt George
Picture Editor: Clara Nicolai
Text Editor: Richard Murphy
Writers: Patricia C. Bangs, Donald Davison Cantlay, Richard
D. Kovar, Brooke Stoddard
Researchers: Harris J. Andrews III, Loretta Y. Britten, Reginald
H. Dickerson, Margaret Gray, Molly McGhee, Alfreda
Robertson, Jayne T. Wise
Copy Coordinators: Ann Bartunek, Allan Fallow, Elizabeth
Graham, Barbara F. Quarmby
Art Assistant: Mikio Togashi
Picture Coordinator: Betty Hughes Weatherley
Editorial Assistant: Constance Strawbridge

Special Contributor: Virginia Baker (translations)

Correspondents: Christine Hinze (London), Christina
Lieberman (New York)

Director of Finance: Christopher Hearing
Directors of Book Production: Marjann Caldwell,
Patricia Pascale
Director of Publishing Technology: Betsi McGrath
Director of Photography and Research: John Conrad Weiser
Director of Editorial Administration: Barbara Levitt
Production Manager: Carolyn Bounds
Quality Assurance Manager: James King
Chief Librarian: Louise D. Forstall

The Author: RUSSELL MILLER, a former British Army
officer, writes for *The Mail on Sunday,* a London news-
paper. He was a contributor on many foreign stories
for *The Sunday Times of London,* and is the author of
another book in the Time-Life Books World War II
series, *The Resistance,* and of *The East Indiamen* in the
Seafarers series. Other books by Russell Miller include
Nothing Less Than Victory and a number of biographies.

The Consultants: COL. JOHN R. ELTING, USA (Ret.),
is a military historian and author of *The Battle of
Bunker's Hill, The Battles of Saratoga* and *Military
History and Atlas of the Napoleonic Wars.* He edited
*Military Uniforms in America: The Era of the American
Revolution, 1755-1795* and *Military Uniforms of
America: Years of Growth, 1796-1851,* and was associ-
ate editor of *The West Point Atlas of American Wars.*

BRIGADIER PETER YOUNG was a British military
historian who commanded the British Army's No. 3
Commando and later the 1st Commando Brigade during World War II. He saw action in some of the major
Commando operations of the War, including the raids
on Guernsey in 1940, Lofoten and Vagsoy in 1941 and
Dieppe in 1942, and the landings in Sicily and Italy
in 1943, Normandy in 1944 and the Arakan in 1944
and 1945, and was awarded the Distinguished Service
Order and the Military Cross. He wrote *Bedouin
Command, Commando* and *Storm from the Sea,* as
well as many other books about Commandos.

R 10 9 8 7 6 5 4 3 2 1

Library of Congress Cataloging-in-Publication Data
Miller, Russell.
  The commandos.

  (World War II)
  Bibliography.
  Includes index.
  1. World War, 1939-1945—Commando operations.
I. Time-Life Books. II. Title. III. Series.
D794.5.M54   940.54'12'41   81-13600
ISBN 0-7835-5710-8

CHAPTERS

PICTURE ESSAYS

CONTENTS

THE STORMING OF EBEN EMAEL

Heading for Fort Eben Emael, the stronghold guarding the eastern frontier of Belgium, German sappers paddle across the Albert Canal in May of 1940.

A BELGIAN FORTRESS OVERCOME BY STEALTH

In 1940, when Adolf Hitler's war machine menaced France and England, both nations hoped that Belgium's Fort Eben Emael—a formidable redoubt on a promontory above the Albert Canal, 15 miles west of the German border—would check a German thrust to the southwest. The fort bristled with two 120mm and sixteen 75mm guns housed in steel-reinforced concrete bunkers, built to withstand the most powerful artillery. Aboveground, the wedge-shaped fort was protected on one side by a rocky cliff that dropped 130 feet straight down to the canal. The other two sides were fringed with minefields, machine guns, barbed-wire entanglements and a moat. Below ground were five miles of tunnels that linked one gun to another and gave cover to the fort's 780 defenders. By the standards of conventional warfare, Eben Emael seemed impregnable.

But before dawn on May 10, 1940, nine gliders swooped over the fort's outer defenses and landed on its grassy roof. The Belgians stared in disbelief as 70 German troopers disembarked and, in 20 minutes, captured 14 of the fort's 18 guns. At the same time other glider groups landed near three bridges that Eben Emael's guns defended, seizing two of the bridges intact. The Belgians at the fort fled below ground to try to defend themselves from within. Only there, and at one bridge, did the Germans meet protracted resistance.

When Fort Eben Emael fell, the main invasion route across Belgium to France lay unobstructed, and the Wehrmacht traveled that way to complete its conquest within the month. For the Allies as well as the Axis, the raid had another significance: It showed that, with special training, stealth and surprise, a diminutive force could overcome one far larger—and pave the way for a major military undertaking. The term "commando" had not yet entered the lexicon of World War II, but the German raiders foreshadowed the techniques in which commandos would specialize, operating both independently and within major campaigns. How the German raiders accomplished their exploit is shown on the following pages in on-the-scene pictures and in clips from a subsequent German film re-creating the raid.

Atop limestone cliffs, Fort Eben Emael overlooks the Albert Canal. The trails connect gun emplacements, which were also linked underground.

Preceded by a flamethrower, German raiders approach a concrete bunker at Fort Eben Emael. Gliders deposited the men within 20 yards of their targets.

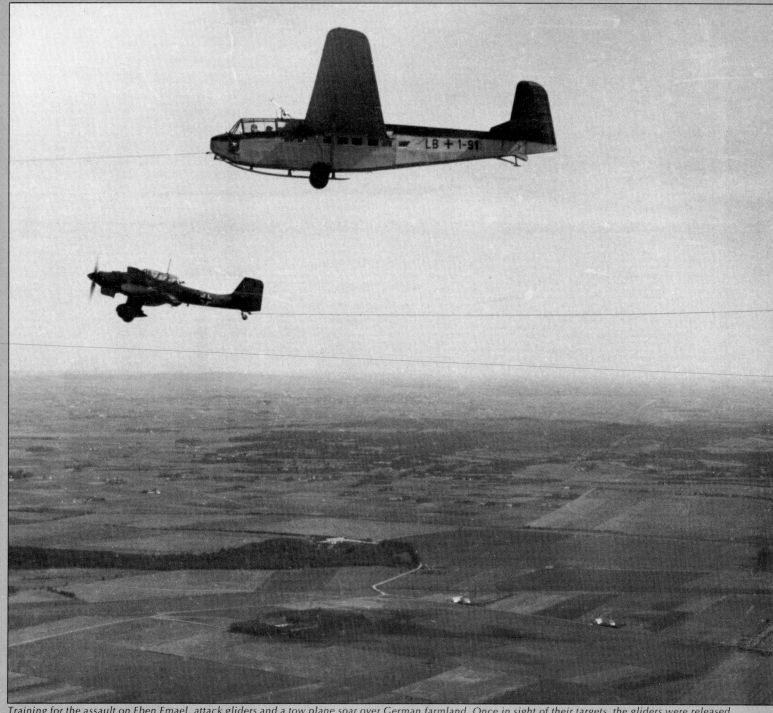

Training for the assault on Eben Emael, attack gliders and a tow plane soar over German farmland. Once in sight of their targets, the gliders were released.

REALISTIC TRAINING ON MOCK TARGETS

One key to the success of the German coup at Fort Eben Emael was the prolonged and rigorous training that preceded the raid. The troops were recruited in November 1939 from among elite parachutists, skilled sappers (demolition specialists) and champion glider sportsmen. For six months they received extraordinarily realistic training.

The raiders practiced on a mock fort that exactly matched the specifications of the real Eban Emael. By lucky coincidence, German subcontractors had been imported to Belgium between 1932 and 1935 to build the fort and had taken its plans home to Germany with them. Moreover, unlike most soldiers of the day, the men training for Eben Emael used real gun emplacements—those along the silenced border of Czechoslovakia.

The training combined attention to detail with calculated flexibility. The men were divided into squads, each with an assigned target. But they also studied targets not their own so that they could back up one another in an emergency. Even the glider pilots learned to fight; once they had landed, they were expected to join their passengers in the assault.

A German soldier makes ready to leap from his glider during a simulation of the planned attack.

An assault team charges past a barbed-wire entanglement. Drill reduced to seconds the time that men needed to spring out of the gliders and into action.

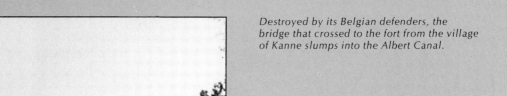

Bypassing the blown-up bridge, German troops lug a rubber boat through Kanne to the Albert Canal. The villagers were so stunned they put up little resistance.

A CANAL CROSSING UNDER FIRE

Against the possibility of a conventional overland approach, the Belgians had laid charges to blow up the three Albert Canal bridges covered by the fort's guns. At two of the bridges the German glidermen took advantage of the shock produced by their unorthodox mode of arrival; they quickly defused the explosives and captured the bridges intact.

However, the third bridge—at Kanne, about a mile northwest of the fort—was set in rough terrain, so the gliders were forced to land some distance from their objective. In the time the Germans spent reaching the bridge, its Belgian defenders ignited a fuse hidden in a nearby road marker and blew up the bridge. When the Germans tried to cross the canal—some working their way single file across the collapsed superstructure of the bridge— a seven-man squad in a bunker at the bridge and other Belgians along the banks of the canal turned their guns on the raiders. The Germans struggled for 10 hours before they were able to overcome the Belgian resistance, seize the bunker and secure the village of Kanne, which lay astride the canal. Now only the fort—already crippled—remained to be cleared.

Stroking through the smoke of Belgian artillery, German troops negotiate the Albert Canal by dinghy.

Their mission accomplished, two German attack gliders rest on the grassy roof of Fort Eben Emael. Barbed wire had been wrapped around the gliders' skids to bring them to a quick stop on landing.

Carrying an explosive on a long pole, a German sapper (top) sneaks across a Belgian bunker at the western approach to Fort Eban Emael. At bottom, the charge explodes after being lowered into a gun embrasure.

In this German re-creation of the assault, a white smoke screen rises above the cliff as reinforcing German troops approach the northern tip of the fort by dinghy.

BEATING BACK A COUNTERATTACK

As the first day of fighting wore on at Fort Eben Emael, the Belgians recovered sufficiently from their surprise to threaten a breakout from the underground passageways into which they had withdrawn, and to challenge the German raiders who occupied the surface of the fort.

But the Germans beat back the Belgian counterattack, and—joined by reinforcements of 50 men early the next morning—terrorized the Belgians by dropping explosives at random down the steep stairways that led from the guns on top to the tunnels below. They also made forays into some of the tunnels, firing deafening, demoralizing volleys down the long passageways.

The Belgians were subdued by the raiders everywhere in the fort except at one western gun emplacement, which overlooked the blown-up bridge from Kanne. The raiders assailed this final bunker with a flamethrower and exploded a charge against the embrasure. That silenced both the gun and its defenders, opening the way for the Germans to enter the interior of Fort Eben Emael unopposed.

TAKING OVER A BATTERED PRIZE

By midmorning on the second day of the assault, nearly a full battalion of Germans ranged practically at will over the grounds and around the walls of Fort Eben Emael. The darkened tunnels under the fort were strewn with dead and wounded. The survivors were so demoralized that many were clamoring for an end to the struggle; even when the commander agreed to surrender, he could not round up all his men. One Belgian officer was discovered ignominiously hiding under a bed.

Shortly after noon on the second day, the Belgians surrendered. The only task that remained for the Germans was to search the fort and tally the haul, which included the 18 big guns. Afterward, the attackers collected their gear and headed for a local inn to relax before boarding trucks to return to Germany.

Carrying the white flag of surrender, a Belgian soldier emerges from the fort on May 11, 1940.

German soldiers survey the grounds near a blasted gun emplacement. After the battle, the Germans turned the fort into a machine shop and a barracks.

Fresh German troops stand about indifferently as wounded Belgians lie on the grass awaiting medical attention. The defenders lost 25 dead, 59 wounded.

Tired and dirty but flushed with success, the Germans enjoy a breather back at their barracks in Germany. Regular troops had replaced them to hold the fort.

Adolf Hitler stands with the officers who led the raid on Eben Emael after personally awarding each of them the Knight's Cross, Germany's highest combat decoration. At a separate ceremony, enlisted men were given the Iron Cross. In addition to receiving medals, all officers and men were promoted one grade in rank. Within weeks of the exploit, the unit that had trained so long for the brief assault was disbanded and its members were scattered throughout the Wehrmacht.

1

On the afternoon of Tuesday, June 4, 1940, Prime Minister Winston Churchill announced to a hushed House of Commons that the remnants of the British Army had been withdrawn from the beaches of Dunkirk "out of the jaws of death and shame." After retreating to the French port on the English Channel, the British forces had narrowly escaped annihilation at the hands of the victorious German Wehrmacht, which was concluding its devastating blitzkrieg of Western Europe. Now France was crushed, and Great Britain stood alone against the formidable German armies. The future was grim.

That evening, as Lieut. Colonel Dudley Clarke, a staff officer at the War Office in Whitehall, walked slowly home through the gathering dusk, he wondered—as people everywhere were wondering that night—what lay in store for Britain. Clarke was an officer with some 20 years' service and a deep interest in military history. And as he strolled, he tried to analyze what other nations had done in the past when their armies were driven from the field.

In the Peninsular War of 1808-1814, he remembered, Spaniards responded to the French aggressors by staging hit-and-run raids behind enemy lines with small bands of lightly armed irregular soldiers referred to as guerrillas. Ninety years later, when Britain invaded the Transvaal in South Africa, marauding bands of the Dutch settlers called Boers fought back with similar raids. In British-occupied Palestine in 1936, Clarke himself had witnessed how a handful of ill-armed Arabs, attacking by surprise and maneuvering superbly, had tied down more than an entire corps of regular British Army troops.

Surely, Clarke thought, Britain might learn from the tactics of Spaniard, Boer and Arab. Before he went to bed that night, he sat down at a desk in his study with a sheet of paper before him. In neat script, he outlined a plan for a new kind of British force cast in the mold of history's guerrilla movements. For want of a better name, he used the one adopted by the Boers. They had called their troops "commandos," from an Afrikaans word meaning military units.

At the War Office next day, Clarke's superior—Sir John Dill, chief of the Imperial General Staff—spoke of the urgency of rekindling the Army's offensive spirit. Clarke produced his one-page outline, and Dill took to the idea as soon as he read it. He promptly passed Clarke's outline on

A NEW BREED OF SOLDIER

to the Prime Minister. Churchill had been thinking along the same lines; he liked Clarke's idea so well that one day later the War Cabinet received a memorandum from him. ''Enterprises must be prepared with specially trained troops of the hunter class who can develop a reign of terror down the enemy coast,'' Churchill wrote. ''I look to the Joint Chiefs of Staff to propose measures for a ceaseless offensive against the whole German-occupied coastline, leaving a trail of German corpses behind.''

Shortly before lunch that day, Sir John Dill asked Clarke to come into his office and told him: ''Your commando scheme is approved, and I want you to get it going at once. Try to get a raid across the Channel mounted at the earliest possible moment.''

Thus was born a breed of fighting men that combined the tactics, independence and resourcefulness of the guerrilla with the training and discipline of the professional soldier. The mixture was destined to produce a military elite: the commandos. Their first task was to steal from the sea to strike, swift and hard, at the bastions of Hitler's Fortress Europe. In ''butcher-and-bolt'' raids along the entire coast of occupied Europe, they killed, captured and destroyed. Gradually, as they acquired special skills that enabled them to graduate from mere hit-and-run raids on coastal outposts, the commandos branched out to extensive operations deep behind enemy lines. In the sand wastes of the North African desert, commando-like units adapted centuries-old Arab survival tactics and dwelt for weeks at a time in the heart of German-held territory. Elsewhere, waterborne commandos mastered the tricks of rough-water canoeing to penetrate alien waterways and sabotage Axis shipping.

Although neither Clarke nor anyone else in England knew it at the time he conceived the idea for the British Commandos, the Germans had independently developed much the same sort of group for a raid on the Belgian fort of Eben Emael (pages 6-19). The Germans disbanded that group when its mission was completed, but later, on the Eastern Front, they would create a more permanent force, called the Brandenburgers after the town in which they trained. Speaking fluent Russian and wearing Red Army uniforms, the Brandenburgers operated entirely behind Soviet lines to frustrate and confound their enemy.

In the West, the example of the British Commandos spawned a host of similar outfits with names of their own, the U.S. Rangers and the Australian Independent Companies among them. And as the momentum of the War gradually shifted in the Allies' favor, the role that these groups played was further expanded to suit Allied strategy. They were called upon to organize and train burgeoning civilian resistance groups in Europe, and later to work with conventional troops in staging major offensives—with the commando groups always in the vanguard of the assault.

No matter what their nationality or allegiance, units of commando-style troops the world over were employed for the most hazardous of the War's tasks. Almost always their members were volunteers. They were romantic, independent, often fanatical, sometimes eccentric, occasionally suicidal. They all knew beforehand that their capture might mean death by firing squad. Facing that ultimate possibility required two exceptional characteristics: outstanding courage and an unquenchable lust for war.

Dudley Clarke took seriously his order to ''get going''; the first British Commando raid was launched in scarcely three weeks. On the night of June 24, four Royal Air Force air-sea rescue boats throbbed across the English Channel toward the coast of France. On board were 115 hastily chosen volunteer soldiers, all of them busily blacking their faces for camouflage. They used make-up that had been supplied by a London theatrical costumier; they found this amusing, and as they applied the blacking they cracked minstrel jokes. Their plan was to land at four points along the French coast south of Boulogne to test the German defenses and take some prisoners.

The timing was propitious. The armistice between Germany and defeated France was due to take effect the following morning. A Commando strike would show the Germans that, notwithstanding the fall of France, Great Britain intended to fight on.

But as a prelude to the offensive demanded by the Prime Minister, the raid was hardly promising. One landing party splashed ashore, blundered around a desolate area of sand dunes in the dark for a while, discovered nothing, encountered no one and duly reembarked. Another boat found that a German seaplane anchorage was straddling its intended landing site, and none of the soldiers on board managed to make it to shore. A third group landed near the town of Le Touquet, surprised two German sentries and killed both of them. But not one of the fledgling Commandos thought to search the bodies, as they had been trained to do, for documents that might have yielded valuable military information. They did not even bother to find out what the sentries were guarding.

The fourth boat, with Clarke on board as an observer, had a faulty compass and very nearly steered straight into German hands. "Suddenly, without the slightest warning," Clarke later wrote, "a searchlight flashed out in the darkness right ahead." They had almost blundered into Boulogne harbor. Hastily they turned back out to sea and resumed the search for their landing site.

When at last they located the right beach, the Commandos slipped over the side and waded ashore. They found nothing but sand dunes. Then, just as they were preparing to reembark, a German patrol appeared on bicycles at the far end of the beach. Major Ronnie Tod was carrying one of the 20 Tommy guns the Commandos had been issued for the

raid. Unfortunately, he had a defective weapon: As he cocked it, the magazine fell off and clattered onto the stony beach. The Germans immediately opened fire. "It is doubtful if they had much to aim at in the darkness," Clarke reported, "but they must have directed it all at the shadow of the boat, for the bullets started to fly around us. Suddenly something caught me a violent blow on the side of the head and sent me headlong to the deck. A moment or two must have passed before I struggled to my feet again, for by then someone was shouting that the Germans were making off."

Clarke had been nicked by a stray bullet that almost severed his ear. No one else was hit, and all of the Commandos got safely back into the boat before German reinforcements arrived on the scene.

The four air-sea rescue boats straggled back across the Channel independently. One of them was refused entry to Folkestone harbor until the identity of its occupants could be established. While the men drifted off the harbor boom, they drank the rum that such boats carried for reviving airmen plucked from chill waters. As a result, many of them were distinctly unsteady on their feet when they were at last allowed ashore. As a final indignity, they were arrested by the military police on suspicion of being deserters. It was not, perhaps, the heroes' welcome they were expecting.

After that debacle, the War Office recognized that special recruiting, training and equipment would be necessary if Churchill's call for a "reign of terror down the enemy coast" was ever to be fulfilled. Circulars were sent to all military commands inviting volunteers for hazardous duty of an undefined nature. Potential recruits were warned they would have to become accustomed to "longer hours, more work and less rest than the regular members of His Majesty's Forces and must also become expert in all military uses of scouting—ability to stalk, to move across any type of country by day or night, silently and unseen, and to live 'off the country' for a considerable period."

The fact is that the qualifications Clarke was looking for were not limited to those listed in the circular. He was seeking men, he wrote, with "a dash of Elizabethan pirate, the Chicago gangster and the frontier tribesman, allied to a professional efficiency and standard of discipline of the best regular soldier."

From Scotland and southern England, Commandos raided the German-occupied coasts of Norway and France between June 1940 and March 1942. Their Norwegian targets were fish-oil factories and Army outposts in the Lofoten Islands and Vagsoy. In France, Commandos struck at beach defenses near Boulogne, an airfield on the island of Guernsey, a radar station near Bruneval and docks in the port of Saint-Nazaire.

The response, from an army smarting after Dunkirk and eager for revenge, was overwhelming. As the applications poured in, a series of secret meetings was held at the London home of Constantia Rumbold, a diplomat's daughter who was helping Clarke as a voluntary worker. There Clarke and other War Office planners thrashed out the organization and role of the Commandos. To maintain security, all of the officers came to the Rumbold home in plain clothes and told the butler who answered the door that they were members of a charity committee.

From the beginning, Clarke was determined to dispense with conventional army rules and regulations. To instill independence and self-reliance, he proposed that Commandos not be provided with barracks or mess-hall rations. Instead, he suggested that each man be given an allowance from the day he joined; thereafter he would be responsible for his own food and lodging. To the surprise of everyone, the War Office agreed. For officers the allotment might be as high as 13 shillings and four pence—not bad money in 1940, when a decent room could be had for six shillings a day. The Commando could lodge as he chose; he might take a hotel room or he might seek other quarters. In the event, so many civilians proved eager to cooperate with the war effort that many a Commando got free room and board with a hospitable family that had a room to spare, then pocketed the full allowance. One Commando remembered, "I was solvent for the rest of the War."

None of Clarke's suggestions pleased the military traditionalists, and the commando concept was bitterly criticized by many officers, who complained that the formation of a so-called elite force would drain the best men from their units. This new organization, they argued, could do nothing that their own units could not.

The second Commando raid seemed to bear out the concerns of the military establishment. The purpose of the raid was to sabotage Le Bourg airfield at Guernsey, in the Channel Islands. The British hoped to prevent its use by the Luftwaffe as a forward fighter base during the German invasion of England that was expected at any moment.

Two destroyers, the *Scimitar* and the *Saladin,* were assigned to carry the raiding party of 32 officers and 107 enlisted men. On the night of July 14, in a choppy sea off the coast of Guernsey, the raiders scrambled down the sides of the destroyers into landing launches. The Commandos' troubles began immediately. Their launches had recently been electrically wired to throw magnetic mines off their trail—but the wiring had the unexpected effect of making the Commandos' compasses wildly inaccurate. As a result one boatload of men headed confidently for their designated beach and found themselves facing the cliffs of Sark, an island seven miles east of Guernsey. Another launch had to turn back because of engine trouble.

Eventually 40 men, under the command of then Lieut. Colonel John Durnford-Slater, made it to shore—but only with difficulty. "I jumped in, armpit-deep," Durnford-Slater later recalled. "A wave hit me on the back of the neck and caused me to trip over a rock. All around me officers and men were scrambling for balance, falling, coming up and coughing salt water. I doubt if there was a dry weapon amongst us. Once on shore, we loosened the straps of our battle dress to let the sea pour out."

After they pulled themselves together, the bedraggled Commandos squelched up a long flight of concrete steps to

Brigadier John Durnford-Slater, leader of several early Commando raids, reflects the quiet self-assurance that carried Commandos through their daring work. "It is the greatest job in the Army," said a fellow officer, adding, "It's revolutionary."

the clifftop and headed for the airfield. They found it completely deserted and clearly unused. The nearby barracks, where they expected to find German troops billeted, was empty. Disconcerted, the Commandos combed the Jerbourg peninsula on the southeast corner of the island; they found nothing. By the time they got back to the beach, the rising swell and the crashing surf had forced their launch to withdraw from the shore. The luckless raiders tried to get out to the launch in a dinghy, but it capsized after only a few trips and smashed to pieces on the rocks. The remaining Commandos had to swim to the launch.

Durnford-Slater was under no illusions about the adventure. "The raid was a ridiculous, almost comic, failure. We had captured no prisoners. We had done no serious damage. We had caused no casualties to the enemy. We had cut through three telegraph cables: A youth in his teens could have done the same. On the credit side, we gained a little experience and learned some of the things not to do."

Despite the comic-opera aspect of those first two raids, Churchill's enthusiasm for the Commandos persisted. On July 17, 1940, Fleet Admiral Sir Roger Keyes was appointed Director of Combined Operations, a new organization established to direct all raiding missions and to coordinate them with Naval and Air Force operations. Keyes was a prickly, opinionated old warrior who had served in the Navy since his youth. He was also Member of Parliament for Portsmouth and had frequently criticized the conduct of the War. But he was extremely popular with the public, to whom he was known as the "hero of Zeebrugge" for a daring raid he had led on the German-held Belgian port of that name in 1918.

Keyes had ambitious plans for the Commandos: He intended to use them in large-scale operations that would gain for them the same kind of glory he had won at Zeebrugge. That was no easy goal, considering the shortage of arms and equipment, but he was optimistic that once his force was assembled, trained and ready to strike, the necessary hardware would be provided. But Keyes underestimated the resentment that the Commandos had provoked. Bureaucrats in the War Office had no intention of catering to this raffish, irregular and unconventional organization. Keyes fumed and thumped tables, but got nowhere.

At that point Churchill stepped in again. He wrote to Anthony Eden, the Secretary of State for War, on August 25. "I hear that the whole position of the Commandos is being questioned," he began. "I thought therefore I might write to let you know how strongly I feel. There will certainly be many opportunities for minor operations, all of which will depend on surprise landings of lightly equipped, nimble forces accustomed to work like packs of hounds instead of being moved about in the ponderous manner which is appropriate to regular formations. For every reason, therefore, we must develop the storm troop, or Commando, idea." In response to Churchill's appeal, Eden issued orders to accelerate the Commando program.

By October 1940, the volunteers, designated the Special Service Brigade, totaled some 2,000 men. As the brigade expanded, it was organized into units called Commandos, and numbered from one to 12. Each Commando was further divided into sections called troops; at full strength, each troop would comprise 50 men. As the War went on, the number of Commando units increased, and the sizes of individual units varied from a handful to more than 100.

The new Commandos threw themselves wholeheartedly into a crash training program of assault courses, speed marches and amphibious landing exercises in camps that were scattered throughout the Scottish Highlands. "Night and day we trained," recalled Peter Young of No. 3 Commando. Each troop would take turns rushing in and out of

Concealing their high hopes with dubious scowls, British Prime Minister Winston Churchill and Sir Roger Keyes, head of the Commandos, review an exercise on a Scottish hillside. Both championed the new hard-hitting special force, but they had trouble getting funds from the War Office.

the landing craft. "Before long," Young said, "30 men, fully armed, could clear one and double up the beach to cover in about 15 seconds."

"There was nothing to do but work," said Durnford-Slater. "We would start on the landing craft at 8 a.m. and follow on with drill, marching, shooting and long schemes on the hills. We also went in for obstacle courses and close combat, which included wrestling and work with knives and pistols, taught by two ex-Shanghai policemen. We learned methods of getting into houses, throwing grenades in front of us and shooting the Tommy guns. A normal day would end at dark, but at least three times a week the men were out at night."

The training was guaranteed to appeal to men of action; but of real action there was no sign. Keyes finally came up with two proposals to make use of his Commandos. The first plan was to seize the Azores; if Spain should fall to the Germans, thus barring the Mediterranean to Allied convoys bound for the Middle East, a base on the Azores would help ensure a safe route via the South Atlantic and the Cape of Good Hope. In high spirits five Commando units began intensive training at Inveraray, in Scotland. But after weeks of tense expectation, they were told that the attack had been indefinitely postponed.

The next plan was to seize Pantelleria, an island between Sicily and Tunisia, to afford the British another Mediterranean base. Keyes persuaded the Prime Minister to give him personal command of the Pantelleria operation, and he was thrilled by the prospect. Two thousand Commandos trained for the raid, and through part of December they were in daily expectation of leaving. But at the last moment the operation was canceled.

The disappointments began to affect morale. The men grumbled, and in the local pubs, drunkenness increased. Said Brigadier J. Charles Haydon, head of the Special Service Brigade, in a report at the time: "A great enthusiasm at the beginning has evaporated, or at least decreased, owing to the repeated postponements of expected events and enterprises. There is a growing irritation with life due partly to these postponements and partly to being harried from pillar to post, onto ships and off them, into billets and out of them, and so on. There is, in short, a sense of frustration."

At last, in February 1941, the commanding officers of Nos. 3 and 4 Commandos were summoned to a meeting at the Marine Hotel in the Scottish town of Troon and briefed on the Lofotens, a group of Norwegian coastal islands well inside the Arctic Circle. Factories in the Lofotens processed herring and cod oil into glycerine that Germany used for manufacturing munitions, and into vitamin A and B pills that supplied the Wehrmacht. The British War Office had decided to send the Commandos to blow the factories up. And this time there was no postponement.

At midnight on March 1, escorted by five destroyers, the raiding force sailed from Scapa Flow at the northern tip of Scotland in two cross-channel steamers, the *Queen Emma* and the *Princess Beatrix*, which had been converted into troop carriers. On board were 500 Commandos, a detachment of Royal Engineers and a platoon of 52 Norwegian volunteers. In the three days of the journey, many of the men suffered from seasickness as the steamers rolled and pitched in the stormy northern waters.

On the night of March 3, the navigation lights of the Lofotens were sighted. At 4 a.m. on March 4, in the pale gray light of dawn, the Commandos lowered their landing craft, loaded them and steered for the shores of the two islands where the factories stood. It was a frigid morning. One officer was bundled up in two undershirts, two pull-overs, a shirt and vest, a wool-lined coat, woolen pants, woolen socks and fur-lined boots, and still he complained about the cold temperature.

Though they saw no sign of enemy activity on the shore, the Commandos had every reason to expect that their landing would be opposed. "We approached the quay fully prepared for an ambush," said Peter Young, in command of No. 6 Troop. "It was a complete anticlimax when crowds of Norwegians of both sexes reached down for our weapons and hoisted us ashore." The reception was welcome nevertheless. The only opposition came from an armed German trawler, the *Krebbs*, which resolutely sailed out alone from the harbor to engage the destroyers. She was quickly set afire and sunk.

The Commandos took over the telegraph station and telephone exchange and began rounding up Germans (mostly merchant seamen) and Norwegian collaborators pointed out to them by the townspeople. The Royal Engineers,

QUICK-FIRING WEAPONS FOR MEN ON THE RUN

For the hit-and-run tactics in which they specialized, Commandos needed a gun that was lightweight, compact and capable of rapid fire. They got those features in the Tommy gun and the Sten (below).

The Tommy gun was the brainchild of General John T. Thompson, who served as a U.S. Army ordnance officer in World War I. He wanted a weapon that could do what the machine gun could do—fire automatically, and thereby mow down a number of men in one burst, but also be portable and manageable by men acting independently on the move. In 1917 he invented such a weapon. It weighed only 12 pounds when loaded. He named his creation the Thompson submachine gun.

Thompson just missed having his gun adopted in World War I, so it languished for a decade—until the mid-1920s, when it was discovered by Chicago gangsters who were vying for the fortune to be had from peddling liquor in defiance of Prohibition. As the weapon gained notoriety in news stories about the gangsters, it became known as the Tommy gun.

Peacetime armies, with no pressing incentive to modernize, were slow to adopt the new gun. As late as 1940, when the first Commando unit was formed, the entire British Army owned only 40 Tommy guns. Each was handmade and, at $225 apiece, the price was steep.

Two engineers, Major Reginald V. Shepherd and Harold J. Turpin of the Royal

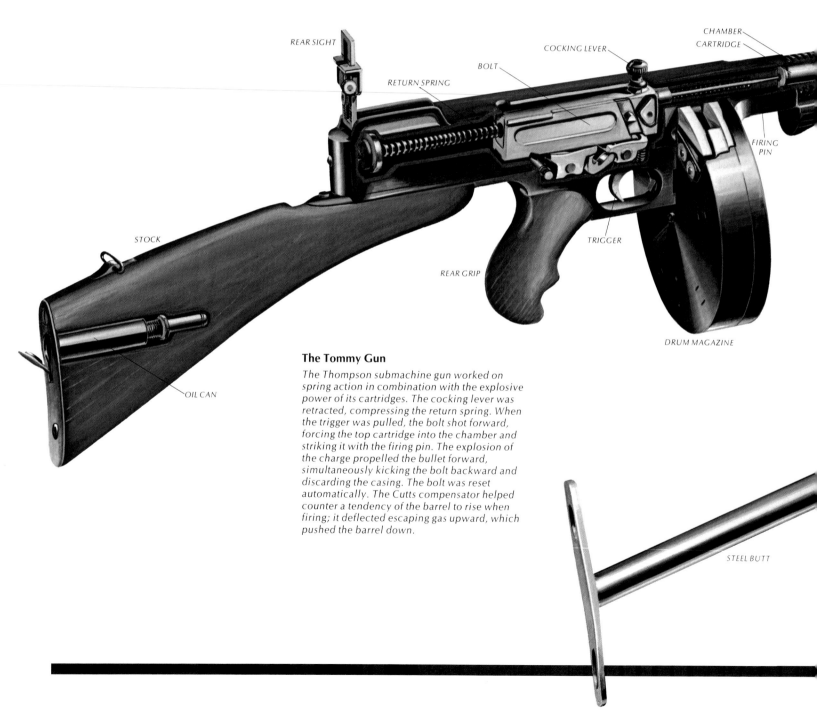

REAR SIGHT • RETURN SPRING • BOLT • COCKING LEVER • CHAMBER • CARTRIDGE • FIRING PIN • STOCK • OIL CAN • REAR GRIP • TRIGGER • DRUM MAGAZINE • STEEL BUTT

The Tommy Gun

The Thompson submachine gun worked on spring action in combination with the explosive power of its cartridges. The cocking lever was retracted, compressing the return spring. When the trigger was pulled, the bolt shot forward, forcing the top cartridge into the chamber and striking it with the firing pin. The explosion of the charge propelled the bullet forward, simultaneously kicking the bolt backward and discarding the casing. The bolt was reset automatically. The Cutts compensator helped counter a tendency of the barrel to rise when firing; it deflected escaping gas upward, which pushed the barrel down.

Small Arms Factory at Enfield, devised an alternative. Their version was shorter by three inches, lighter by four pounds and lacked such frills as a hideaway oil can. Not the least of its virtues was that it consisted of a mere 24 parts and could be mass-produced for less than $15. The gun came to be known as the Sten, an acronym that combined the initials of its inventors' last names with the first two letters of Enfield. Before long, British Commandos and their counterparts in the other forces were armed with Stens or with close imitations.

The Drum Magazine

The magazine of the Thompson submachine gun contained a coiled spring that propelled up to 50 cartridges in a spiral to an opening at the top; then the bolt pushed the cartridges into the gun. When the magazine was empty it was replaced by a full one, and the spring was recoiled by means of the winding key.

The Sturdy Sten

The Sten gun operated in essentially the same way as the Thompson. The bolt pushed the cartridge into the chamber just below the front sight, and the firing pin struck the rear of the cartridge. After the powder exploded, the bolt compressed the return spring and the cartridge casing flew out through the ejection port. The firing action continued until the trigger was released or the cartridges were spent. The box magazine, which was less expensive to make than the drum type, fed 32 cartridges into the chamber. The barrel sleeve, which was perforated with ventilation holes for cooling the chamber area, served as a hand grip.

meanwhile, went methodically about their business. Ear-shattering explosions were followed by clouds of billowing black smoke as 18 fish-oil factories blew up, along with storage tanks containing 800,000 gallons of fuel oil. Five small merchant ships were destroyed by the resulting fire. At the telegraph station, Commando Lieutenant R. L. Wills sent off a telegram addressed to A. Hitler, Berlin: "You said in your last speech German troops would meet the English wherever they landed. Where are your troops?"

Soon after midday, the soldiers returned to their boats; as the landing craft moved out of the harbor, the townspeople—delighted by the raid though it had destroyed their chief source of livelihood—gathered on the quay and sang the Norwegian anthem. Some 314 of them, including eight women, had volunteered to return with the Commandos to Great Britain to join the Norwegian forces that had fled there in April 1940 rather than surrender to the Germans. Also on board were 216 German prisoners. The only injury the British had sustained during the entire raid was incurred by an officer who accidentally shot himself in the thigh with an automatic he carried in his pants pocket.

Peter Young, shown here as a colonel and wearing the Commando green beret, fought as a second lieutenant in the first Commando raid, on Guernsey in 1940, and took part in a score of later operations from Norway to Burma—more than any other Commando.

The raid had been an unalloyed success, but a crisis was brewing for Sir Roger Keyes. In April 1941 the Prime Minister approved plans for Commandos to occupy the Canary Islands to protect British convoys en route to the South Atlantic. However, weeks turned into months and there was no sign of the operation getting started. Every day Keyes became more resentful of what he viewed as needless procrastination by War Office bureaucrats.

In August, a demonstration landing exercise was scheduled at Scapa Flow for the edification of King George VI. The exercise was a fiasco. Communications failed, the beach became choked with equipment and the men exhibited precious little of their touted élan. The raid on the Canaries was indefinitely postponed.

By this time, relations between Keyes and the commanders of the Naval and military forces had deteriorated seriously; Keyes even began complaining that junior officers in the Admiralty were plotting against him. At the end of September, Keyes's title was changed from Director of Combined Operations to "Adviser"—a move calculated to enrage the gallant admiral. He declined the post, indignantly telling the Prime Minister that he could not accept "such a sweeping reduction in status."

Keyes, still a Member of Parliament, stood before the House of Commons and delivered a bitter farewell message in which he spoke of "having been frustrated in every worthwhile offensive action I have tried to undertake," and railed against "the negative power which controls the war machine in Whitehall. Great leaders of the past have always emphasized the value of time in war: Time is passing and so long as procrastination, the thief of time, is the key word of the war machine in Whitehall, we shall continue to lose one opportunity after another during the lifetime of opportunities."

Churchill's choice as a replacement for Keyes both surprised and delighted the Commandos: Captain Lord Louis Mountbatten (pages 168-179). He was a man as likely as Keyes to arouse passions, but for different reasons. Rich, handsome, a cousin of the King, a fine polo player and a member of fashionable London society, Mountbatten was thought by some to be a playboy and dilettante. But to others he was a brave Naval officer and a gifted leader who almost invariably aroused the admiration of subordinates. He

From a quay in the Norwegian Lofoten Islands, three British Commandos watch as fish-oil storage tanks burn in March 1941. Factories in the Lofotens produced half of Norway's fish oil—and processed much of it into glycerine for the manufacture of German explosives.

also had the ability—and the contacts—to cut through red tape and get things done.

Captain Mountbatten had recently returned from the Mediterranean, where he had narrowly survived the sinking of his destroyer, the *Kelly*. Now, as Chief of Combined Operations, he was promoted to Acting Vice Admiral of the Royal Navy and given the honorary ranks of Lieutenant General in the Army and Air Marshal in the Royal Air Force. The new titles were more than mere glitter; they underscored the necessity of involving Great Britain's three military services as support forces for Commando operations on a large scale.

Interservice cooperation was put to the test in December in the first big Combined Operations raid of the War—at Vagsoy, an island off the Norwegian coast between the ports of Trondheim and Bergen. The purpose of the raid, like that of the attack on the Lofotens, was mainly economic—to destroy fish-oil factories and merchant shipping. But unlike the Lofotens, Vagsoy was heavily fortified with coastal batteries and German garrisons, and thus there was little possibility of an unopposed landing. The plan was for one group of Commandos to attack and hold the village of South Vagsoy

long enough for another to blow up the factories. But first the coastal guns and antiaircraft batteries on Maloy, a tiny island protecting the channel between Vagsoy and the Norwegian mainland, had to be silenced.

An essential component of the operation was the close cooperation of both the Royal Navy and the Royal Air Force. As the Commandos were going in, Hampden bombers would attack nearby German-occupied airfields, and a cruiser and four destroyers would bombard German artillery positions on Vagsoy and Maloy. During the raid, Blenheims and Beaufighters were to provide cover. The raiding force was made up of 576 men from Nos. 2 and 3 Commandos along with engineers, medics and a Norwegian detachment. The date was set for December 26, 1941, when the Germans might be resting after Christmas festivities.

Mountbatten went to Scapa Flow to wish the raiders good luck. "This is my first experience in telling people what to do in an action without going in myself," he told the Commandos, "and I don't like it." He went on to say that when his destroyer had gone down off Crete a few months earlier the Germans had machine-gunned the survivors in the water. "There is absolutely no need to treat the Germans gently on my account," he said. "Good luck to you all."

worked. About midnight on the 27th of February, 10 of the planes arrived over the drop zone without interference from German antiaircraft fire, and the parachutists began hurling themselves into the clear, cold night. Most of the men landed right on target. Only two planes were forced off course by enemy flak, and these aircraft dropped their parachutists about a mile away on the side of the gully across from the radar station.

Frost decided not to wait for these men to catch up, and ordered an immediate attack. Splitting into four teams, the parachutists raced across the moonlit fields. Frost's team was to storm the villa next to the radar station, where the majority of the German technicians were thought to be housed. Another team headed directly for the station, which sat in a shallow depression between the villa and the cliffs. A third team took up positions to defend against a possible attack by a German garrison known to be billeted in La Presbytère, a large farm to the north, while a fourth team went to clear the gully in preparation for the withdrawal.

By an extraordinary stroke of luck, only one German sentry was awake as the raiders approached the villa. By the time he had run to the barracks to wake the sergeant of the guard, the leading parachutists were on the doorstep. Frost's group burst into the villa and found only one man inside. The raiders killed him as he fumbled for a gun. Leaving a

few men to hold the villa, Frost hurried on to the radar station, where he found that five of the six Germans inside had already been killed. The sixth was captured as he ran toward the cliff edge.

Heavy machine-gun fire opened up from the direction of the farm as Flight Sergeant Cox, apparently unperturbed by the hail of bullets ricocheting around him, began dismantling the radar equipment; it was still warm after tracking the aircraft in which the visitors had arrived. Two bullets hit parts of the equipment while it was actually in Cox's hands, but he calmly continued with his work. Engineers used crowbars to wrench the last components from their mountings, then the equipment was loaded onto a collapsible handcart that had been dropped with the raiders. Heaving and pushing the heavily laden cart as they went, the raiders began to withdraw across the fields toward the gully. Before the last man had departed, the radar station was blown up to make the Germans believe that the purpose of the raid had been sabotage.

The lights of German trucks could be seen coursing down a road toward La Presbytère as the parachutists hurried away. Time was now of the essence. If the gully had been cleared, the paratroopers would be able to make their escape. But the team assigned that job was undermanned and too weak to attack. Most of its members had been in the

British paratroopers search two Germans captured in the raid on the Bruneval radar station. The prisoner on the right, a Luftwaffe radar operator, was taken to England to help explain the German detection equipment; the prisoner on the left is an infantryman.

planes that were forced off course, and these parachutists were still struggling across country toward the gully. Fortunately, they arrived in the nick of time; despite their long and exhausting forced march, they joined their teammates in storming a pillbox overlooking the beach and clearing the last obstacle to the escape.

On the beach, Frost signaled out to sea with a flashlight. After an agonizing wait, he heard a voice in the dark call out: "Sir! The boats are coming in. God bless the ruddy Navy." First to go on board the landing craft was the radar equipment, followed by the paratroopers. Under intermittent fire from machine-gun posts along the cliffs—the German trucks had delivered men to the defenses—the ships headed out to sea.

The whole force, escorted by destroyers (and covered by Spitfires after dawn broke), arrived back in England at midmorning. The raiders had lost one man killed and seven missing; a further five were wounded. With the new German equipment in their hands, British scientists were able to devise countermeasures that were to save countless aircraft—and fliers—during the stormy years that lay ahead.

The success of the Vagsoy and Bruneval raids reflected the growing competence of the commandos and provided an inestimable morale boost for the Allies, who saw little else going right in the War. The latest commando exploits served to sweep away the controversy that had marked the force's inception; now even British Army traditionalists recognized its value, and a special school for Commandos was opened at Achnacarry, Scotland, where training was expanded and centralized (pages 58-73).

The Commandos also impressed the Army of the United States, which had entered the War the previous December. One American admirer was Lucian K. Truscott Jr., then a brigadier general attached to Mountbatten's Combined Operations Headquarters. In the spring of 1942, after a close study of the training at Achnacarry, Truscott suggested to Brigadier General Dwight D. Eisenhower, then assistant chief of staff in charge of War operations, that the Americans follow the British lead and create a commando outfit of their own. His suggestion was quickly approved.

It fell to Truscott to choose a name for the new special force. Since the word "commando" belonged to the British,

Truscott selected "Rangers" after the Colonial guerrillas who had fought the French and the Indians in the French and Indian War of 1755-1763.

A call for volunteers "not averse to dangerous action" from the U.S. 34th Infantry Division and 1st Armored Division, stationed in Northern Ireland, produced an overwhelming response. Nearly 500 candidates were selected, and the first U.S. Rangers arrived at Achnacarry on June 1, 1942, to begin training. To the undisguised surprise of some of the British instructors, the Yanks acquitted themselves with great credit.

The British Army Commandos had also picked up a home-grown rival: the Royal Marine Commandos. One of the original functions of the Marines had been to provide detachments for amphibious raids on enemy coastlines. After Dunkirk, however, they could not be spared for cross-Channel forays: As one of the few British fighting formations with knowledge of amphibious warfare, they had to be kept available for defense against an anticipated German invasion. Then, once the threat of invasion had abated, the Royal Marines found that their original role had been usurped by the Army Commandos.

As early as February 1942, the Marines had begun to emulate the Commandos. One call for Royal Marine volunteers for Commando training produced 6,000 men; they were organized in two units, Nos. 40 and 41 Royal Marine Commandos. Within the year, the entire Marine division would be retrained for service as Commandos. This transformation engendered a fierce rivalry between the Marine and Army Commandos, and that rivalry would last for the entire War.

Through the winter and spring of 1942 the Allies were rocked by one setback after another. In the North African deserts, the British Eighth Army was losing ground to a resurgent German Afrika Korps. In the Far East the Japanese were sweeping into Hong Kong and through Malaya to the great citadel of Singapore. In the Philippines, General Douglas MacArthur, commander of the U.S. forces in the Far East, was fighting a losing battle to hold the islands. And in the North Atlantic, German U-boats were exacting an awesome toll on Allied shipping.

In late January of 1942, the 45,000-ton German battleship *Tirpitz* was lurking in the deep waters of the German-occupied Norwegian fjords, giving every sign of preparing to sortie against Allied convoys in the Atlantic. If she did so, she could deprive both Britain and the Soviet Union of vital supplies. On January 25, Churchill noted in a memo to his Chiefs of Staff that no other target was as important as the *Tirpitz*. "The whole strategy of the war," he wrote, "turns at this period on this ship, which is holding four times the number of British capital ships paralysed, not to speak of two new American battleships retained in the Atlantic."

The *Tirpitz* could operate in the Atlantic only if she had a base of operations along the Atlantic coast of Europe. Such a haven was provided by the French port of Saint-Nazaire,

where a huge dry dock had been built before the War to accommodate the liner *Normandie*. If the *Tirpitz* could be denied the use of this dock, the only one in France big enough, she was unlikely to venture out of North Sea waters.

The chance to stalemate the *Tirpitz* in Norway triggered the most daring and dangerous raid ever planned in Mountbatten's Combined Operations Headquarters. On the night of March 27, 1942, a flotilla of darkened vessels entered the estuary of the Loire River, heading for the Naval base at Saint-Nazaire. On board the leading vessel, Motor Gunboat 314, were the joint commanders of the operation, Lieut. Colonel Charles Newman of No. 2 Commando and Captain

Major General Lucian K. Truscott Jr., who founded the American Rangers, wears riding breeches—signifying his membership in the cavalry—as he observes exercises at the British Commando training center in Scotland.

American Rangers inspect mock graves at the Commandos' training grounds in Achnacarry, Scotland. The inscription on the tombstone at left cautions against walking in front of a fellow Commando's rifle.

Robert "Red" Ryder of the Royal Navy. Before the night was out, both would earn the Victoria Cross. Behind MGB-314 was an old American destroyer, the *Campbeltown,* with a force of 75 Commandos on board. The *Campbeltown's* funnels had been cut back to disguise her as a German *Möwe*-class destroyer, and her bow was packed with explosives. In the forthcoming drama, the *Campbeltown* was to play the leading role: Her assignment was to ram the steel gates of the *Normandie* dock and blow them to bits by means of a delayed explosion.

On either side of the destroyer, in columns along its port and starboard, were 16 mahogany-hulled motor boats car-

rying some 200 more Commandos. Because of the length of the proposed journey, each boat was carrying extra fuel in tanks lashed to its deck. The auxiliary fuel tanks made the wood boats extremely vulnerable in the event of an attack, but no other craft were available for the operation. The planners were hoping that the element of surprise would safeguard the men on board, but no one had any illusions about the risks. During planning, a senior Naval officer had warned Mountbatten: "We may lose every man." With a slight grimace, Mountbatten had agreed, but added, "If they do the job, we've got to accept that."

Shortly before midnight, the raiders heard the approach

AUDACIOUS ASSAULT ON A NORWEGIAN ISLAND

As Combined Operations planned it, the Commando raid on the German-occupied Norwegian island village of South Vagsoy in December of 1941 was to be an audacious frontal assault on a position bristling with heavy guns. Navy and fighter cover were to keep the Commandos' landing craft from being shot out of the water. Many of the Commandos were to land at rugged spots where the Germans would least expect attack. Indeed, when Admiral Sir John Tovey, Commander in Chief of the Home Fleet, saw that one group was scheduled to anchor its 10-ton craft near the base of a cliff, he warned the Commandos that they might have to swim the last leg of their trip in frigid Norwegian waters. The Commandos later boasted that they had landed without even getting their feet wet.

The smooth landing was only the first of the Commandos' triumphs. In fact, the Vagsoy raid was so carefully planned, so thoroughly rehearsed and so deftly executed that it won praise from its earlier advocates and doubters alike. "Even our old enemies at the War Office applauded," one officer remembered. The London *Times*, ordinarily the most restrained of commentators, trumpeted Vagsoy as "the perfect raid." And Captain Peter Young, who led one of the Commando groups ashore, unashamedly pronounced it "a minor classic of amphibious warfare, which despite the multitudinous accidents inseparable from warfare actually went according to plan." In the space of a seven-hour Arctic winter day, the Commandos achieved every tactical objective: They destroyed the protective gun battery on the nearby islet of Maloy, defeated seasoned German garrisons, demolished all the factories at South Vagsoy and, in the opinion of Captain Young, "made a total mess of everything on the island."

Hoping for as much, and needing a success to bolster public morale in that bleak Christmas season of 1941, the War Office had made room in the troop transports for three photographers—one from Movietone News and two from the Army. The photographers returned with dramatic pictures that documented the historic raid minute by minute.

In the cramped quarters belowdecks on a troop transport bound for Vagsoy, Commandos while away the time by arming grenades with fuses.

"Our
said
who
had
Th
the
seco
Fjor
lowe

Plunging through the smoke screen laid down by RAF bombers to obscure the landing from the Germans, Commandos race up the beach at Vagsoy.

KNOCKING OUT A FORTIFIED ROCK

Before the Commandos could hope to secure South Vagsoy, they had to capture the islet of Maloy, a 250-square-yard rock less than 200 yards east of the village. The Germans had taken advantage of the islet's strategic location in the middle of Vags Fjord by emplacing four 75mm guns there to cover the only approach. "The idea of steaming straight into the mouths of four guns firing point-blank," said one Commando, "lacked charm."

But just as the plan prescribed, the *Kenya*, the Navy's lead ship, rained 6-inch shells on the rock; within 20 minutes it had silenced the battery. When 105 Commandos went ashore, they found a German officer and 15 soldiers huddling in an underground shelter, ready to surrender.

The remaining 200 Commandos went on to South Vagsoy; the *Kenya* anchored south of the islet and coordinated the actions of the two groups by radio.

From a hilltop above demolished German barracks on Maloy, a British scout looks across the fjord at the action in South Vagsoy. The bombing of the village was so intense that Commandos offshore saw "huts bursting into flame and being hurled into the air."

Radio operators inform the *Kenya* that Maloy has been taken. Messages to the ship, keeping the commanding officers informed of progress on both islands, averaged one every 90 seconds at the peak of the operation.

Commandos comb Maloy for German survivors. Two Germans were so shell-shocked they had to be half-dragged from a ruin. "They looked very miserable," a Commando said. "I almost felt sorry for them."

Advancing past two halted comrades, a Commando runs up a snow-covered road toward Vagsoy from the distant point at which his unit had landed.

"STICKY" GOING AGAINST A RESOLUTE FOE

"I don't know what we're getting into, but it looks pretty sticky," a British officer cautioned his men as they entered South Vagsoy. What they were getting into was a bitter contest, for despite the pummeling the village had taken, the Germans had dug in and intended to put up a fight.

In the first rush into the village, only one of the British officers survived unscathed. One captain, looking "wild and dangerous," according to the account of his admiring commanding officer, "waded in, shouting and cheering his men, throwing grenades into each house as he came to it and firing from the hip" until the enemy gunned him down.

The Germans took up defensive positions wherever they could inside the buildings in the village, but when the Commandos stormed their redoubts with grenades, incendiary bombs, gasoline torches and a 3-inch mortar, the Germans had to choose between being taken captive, shot down or burned alive.

As soon as the Commandos had secured the village, their demolition teams turned to the targets they had come to destroy: the fish-oil and canning factories. After charges were set, each team leader blew a whistle, the signal for every man to hit the ground—which within seconds was shuddering from the explosions.

Watchful for hidden Germans, three Commandos steal around the corner of a Vagsoy house

Commandos pull a sled loaded with heavy 3-inch shells and a
mortar toward the center of South Vagsoy, where the Germans were
headquartered and where the bloodiest fighting occurred.

destruction of a frame canning factory used by the Germans. A Commando marveled at "the courage of the photographers, who never roamed far from the leading soldiers."

Clutching a white flag of surrender, a German officer leads his men to the beach under close guard by the British. A Commando proudly noted that the raid garnered 98 prisoners, "the first reasonably large collection of German prisoners to be taken to Britain in the War."

MOPPING UP
AND GETTING OUT FAST

Their goals accomplished, the Commandos began to withdraw to their ships. They were beset by German planes that broke through the RAF fighter cover, but again teamwork prevailed. "The Naval escort let fly with everything," a captain said, "keeping the planes at a good height."

In addition to their German captives, the Commandos headed home with a cluster of Norwegians who had asked to be evacuated. Aboard ship, the Norwegians and the raiders sang Christmas carols.

The Commandos had discovered a new pride in themselves. "We had an enthusiastic welcome from the Navy, who until then had held the Army in low esteem since they continually had to rescue and evacuate it," a Commando said. "Things were different now."

A British officer inspects a German field gun on Maloy, destroyed by shelling and demolition.

Commandos trundle a wounded comrade
up the icy slopes of South Vagsoy to an aid post
established near the beach. Sniper fire made
this duty perilous, and one Commando
reported seeing a medical corpsman "first
attending to his wounded, then seizing their
rifles to get a few shots at the enemy."

Dragging a bandaged leg, a Commando
clutches two medical orderlies for support as he
struggles toward a landing craft. Of the
British wounded, six died on the return trip and
were buried at sea. Miraculously, in all the
cross fire only one civilian was killed.

Commandos and three generations of Vagsoy citizens crowd the railing of their transport for a first glimpse of the English coast. Some civilians left Norway for fear of Nazi reprisals, others to join resistance forces in Britain. A Norwegian-born Commando who fought at South Vagsoy said the raid was "the fulfillment of our dreams."

Commandos ready some of the prisoners taken during the raid for interrogation belowdecks. Many Germans who fought at Vagsoy were not so lucky. A German general who arrived on the island to survey the damage the day after the raid found 150 for whom graves would have to be dug; another 41 were missing in action.

RUGGED QUEST FOR THE GREEN BERET

Lieut. Colonel Charles Vaughan, head of British Commando training, confers with Major William Darby of the U.S. Rangers in July 1942.

The success of the raid on Vagsoy *(pages 42-57)* established beyond doubt the validity of the commando idea. The next step, Prime Minister Winston Churchill told Combined Operations Chief Lord Louis Mountbatten as the year 1942 dawned, was to train enough men in the innovative hit-and-run techniques "to keep the whole of the enemy coastline on the alert, from the North Cape to the Bay of Biscay."

Mountbatten's staff promptly established a Commando Basic Training Centre at Achnacarry Castle, seat of the Scottish Clan of Cameron, rented to the government by Sir Donald Cameron, head of the clan. At Achnacarry, in the Highlands, the murky moors, the sheer cliffs, the deep and icy streams and the broad, rock-rimmed lakes provided terrain as bedeviling as any to be found in enemy territory.

To direct the training, the War Office chose Lieut. Colonel Charles Vaughan, a former drill sergeant in the Coldstream Guards and more recently the deputy commander of No. 4 Commando, the group that had participated in the successful raid on the Lofoten Islands in March 1941. Vaughan had "a rugged determination to exact the last ounce from his trainees," one Commando leader observed. "He knew exactly what he wanted and how to get it."

Vaughan devised a grueling 12-week course that turned out tough, self-reliant graduates who could fire a gun accurately on the run, kill silently with a knife or garrote, climb mountains and cross rivers with a few lengths of rope, or march 15 miles in two hours and 15 minutes. Any whose nerves or muscles failed these tests were sent back to their units. The training was realistic in the extreme; in many exercises live ammunition was used, and some 40 recruits were killed at Achnacarry during the War.

But Allied commanders counted results, not costs, and so did aspiring Commandos. So many volunteers signed up that hundreds had to be turned away. Eventually 25,000 Allied soldiers—French and American as well as British—completed the course. The mark of graduation was a green beret, which came to be much coveted. With it grew a spirit of brotherhood that long outlasted the assault courses.